Beating Bullying at Home and in Your Community

Clara MacCarald

Rosen
YA™
New York

To my wife, Laura, and daughter, Hazel

Published in 2018 by The Rosen Publishing Group, Inc.
29 East 21st Street, New York, NY 10010

First Edition

Library of Congress Cataloging-in-Publication Data

Names: MacCarald, Clara, 1979– author.
Title: Beating bullying at home and in your community / Clara MacCarald.
Description: New York, NY : Rosen Publishing, 2018 | Series: The LGBTQ+ guide to beating bullying | Audience: Grades 7–12. | Includes bibliographical references and index.
Identifiers: LCCN 2016056449 | ISBN 9781508174240 (library bound book) | ISBN 9781508174226 (pbk. book) | ISBN 9781508174233 (6 pack)
Subjects: LCSH: Bullying—United States—Prevention—Juvenile literature. | Sexual minority youth—United States—Juvenile literature. | Cyberbullying—United States—Prevention—Juvenile literature.
Classification: LCC BF637.B85 M22 2018 | DDC 302.34/30866—dc23
LC record available at https://lccn.loc.gov/2016056449

Manufactured in the United States of America

CONTENTS

While society has become more accepting of the LGBTQ+ community, **LGBTQ+ kids are** bullied more often than their straight counterparts. Bullying makes schools, homes, and the larger community feel unsafe. All teens deserve a safe and supportive environment, whatever their identity.

LGBTQ+ stands for lesbian, gay, bisexual, transgender, queer or questioning, and more. More might include terms like asexual and intersex. All those terms cover a diverse group of people. What LGBTQ+ people share is a

These people marched in support of same-sex marriage in Australia in 2015. Around the world, people are fighting for the rights of sexual and gender minorities.

sexual orientation, gender identity, or gender expression that is in the minority.

Sexual orientation, or sexuality, is who someone is attracted to. It's not always about sex. The attraction may be primarily romantic or emotional. Gender identity is the gender someone sees themselves as. Gender expression is the way they show their gender to the world through aspects like their name, clothes, hair, and behavior.

L, *G*, and *B* stand for different sexual orientations. The term "lesbian" describes people who identify as female and who are attracted to other females. The word "gay" means attracted to the same gender, although it tends to be used more for people who identify as male. "Bisexual" means attracted to more than one gender.

The next letter, *T* stands for "transgender." It refers to diverse identities. People who are transgender have a gender identity or expression that doesn't match the gender they were assigned at birth. Transgender people may identify as male or female. They may also identify as neither or some combination of both. Transgender people may alter their body or their life to conform to a specific gender, or they may not.

People may embrace other identities if their gender expression or identity does not match what society expects. They may identify as genderqueer, gender fluid, gender nonconforming, or something else. The word "genderqueer" means identifying as neither male nor female or as some combination of the two. The term "gender fluid" describes a gender identity that changes over time. People using these terms may or may not see themselves as transgender. The word "cisgender" means someone whose identity matches the gender they were assigned at birth.

The letter *Q* can stand for "queer" or for "questioning." People may use the word "queer" to mean nonstraight, or it may refer to the entire LGBTQ+ community. A questioning person may be exploring their sexuality, their gender, or both.

And then there's that plus sign at the end. The plus sign makes room for more sex and gender minorities. For example, intersex, asexual, or pansexual. A person who is intersex was born with physical characteristics of both sexes. People who are asexual are not interested in sex, even if they are romantically or emotionally attracted to other people. Pansexual people feel their sexual attraction to others is not limited to any gender.

People may identify with more than one letter in LGBTQ+. For example, a person who is transgender may also question their sexuality. Whether you fit into the LGBTQ+ community, and how, is up to you. Other people can help you figure things out. However, no one gets to define your identity for you. Nor do they have the right to attack you for that identity.

CHAPTER ONE

BULLYING IN THE HOME AND BEYOND

E ven if you haven't experienced bullying yourself, you probably know someone who has. Bullies often target people they see as different. That difference may be due to race, religion, abilities, or other traits like sexuality and gender.

Bullying affects LGBTQ+ teens, or those perceived to be LGBTQ+, more than their straight-seeming peers. According to a 2016 study by the Centers for Disease Control (CDC) 34.2 percent of lesbian, gay, and bisexual high school students reported that they had been bullied on school property over the last year, versus 18.8 percent of straight students. Bullies also target questioning students. According to the same study, 24.9 percent of students unsure of their sexuality reported being bullied.

What Is Bullying?

Simply put, bullying is a series of aggressive acts meant to harm another person. Bullying can be physical, verbal, written, or social. Social bullying damages a person's reputation or relationships. Isolated cruelty, while upsetting, is not bullying. A fair fight doesn't count, either. Bullying requires a power imbalance. That doesn't mean the bully has to be stronger. They might be more popular or better able to influence people.

Unfortunately, sometimes bullies can make themselves more well liked by picking on those they perceive as different.

Other teens might think their behavior is funny, or the teens may want to stay on the bully's good side to avoid being targeted themselves. Bullies enjoy having power and control over other people.

In general, bullying has become less physical, but attacks still happen. According to a 2012–2013 survey by the Gay, Lesbian, and Straight Education Network (GLSEN), one in five LGBT students reported being physically attacked at school. A third were physically harassed. Bullies may also destroy someone's belongings or threaten them with violence.

Physically assaulting someone is only one type of bullying. Keeping someone socially isolated or attacking them in texts or on the internet are other forms of bullying.

Nowadays, a lot of bullying is verbal. Words wielded with the intent to harm can cause great damage. A relentless barrage of negative comments and insults can wear someone down until they feel bad about themselves. Bullies often act in front of an audience. A bully might out someone's sexuality or gender identity without their permission.

Bullies may start a campaign of social exclusion against someone. They may spread rumors and encourage others to shun their victim. They may manage to keep a teen from being invited to a social event that everyone else is attending or keep them from joining groups.

Even when antibullying policies are in place, many of these policies don't specifically mention LGBTQ+ issues. Bullies can think LGBTQ+ teens are fair game. Victims assume adults will not try to stop the harassment.

Bullying takes its toll. It makes targets feel isolated and lonely. Teens may miss class, especially if their bullies go to the same school. Their grades may drop because of the stress. Bullied teens are more likely to suffer from anxiety, depression, and other mental health problems. They may harm themselves through substance abuse or engage in risky behavior.

Toxic Families

Many LGBTQ+ kids have supportive families. The Human Rights Campaign (HRC), an organization that works for LGBTQ+ civil rights, polled self-identified lesbian, gay, bisexual, and transgender teens in 2012. Two thirds of the teens said their family was accepting of LGBT people. But 33 percent of the

Teens who are overwhelmed by bullying may turn to drugs or alcohol to feel better, but substance abuse creates its own problems.

teens' families were not accepting. Sometimes one family member is particularly homo- or transphobic. Someone who is homophobic fears or is biased against people who are attracted to the same sex. Someone who is transphobic fears or is biased against transgender people.

Usually bullying is used to label acts that happen between school-aged people, but parents and other caregivers can harass

Parents won't always agree with everything their teen does, but parents who constantly scold or berate their kids are bullies.

kids in similar ways. Such bullying may qualify as maltreatment or child abuse. Physical attacks that cause even minor injuries constitute physical abuse. Verbal attacks, threats, and emotional rejection can qualify as emotional abuse. In 2016, Child Protective Services (CPS) found that 6.3 out of 1,000 youths aged eleven to seventeen were maltreated by caregivers in 2014.

Parents and caregivers have power not only because they are older, but also because of their position in a youth's life. If all a teen hears is a constant stream of negativity from a parent, it tells them that they're not valued or accepted. They may begin to believe the criticisms and insults. If they're constantly being blamed for things going wrong, they may begin to accept being at fault.

Although parental bullying may not be related to LGBTQ+ issues, it can be. Parents may make negative comments whenever they see someone who is LGBTQ+. They may constantly criticize their teen's gender expression. They may invade their kid's privacy because they don't trust them.

They may try to control an LGBTQ+ teen, thinking they can make their offspring straight. These parents disrespect their child's personal decisions. They may forbid them from expressing their gender the way they want to. Parents may control their teen's wardrobe if they are still the ones buying clothes for the family. If the child is out about their identity to their parents, parents may pressure them to stay closeted in public. If they have LGBTQ+ friends, the parent may try to keep them from these allies. Parents may stop their teen from attending LGBTQ+ events.

WHEN HOME ISN'T SAFE

Being harassed by your own family can make you feel like you have nowhere safe to go. Some teens decide their only option is to leave home. But leaving a toxic family brings its own challenges.

Finding supportive foster families can be difficult for LGBTQ+ teens. Teens who want to live on their own must find affordable housing and a job with a decent wage. These challenges make it hard to finish school. Unfortunately, some teens who leave their family become homeless.

Homeless teens may end up living on the street. To avoid this, they might find shelter in housing run by organizations that serve homeless populations. In 2011 and 2012, the Palette Fund surveyed organizations that serve homeless youth. About 40 percent of the youth using these programs were identified as LGBT. Almost half of that 40 percent said they ran away because their family rejected them. Others had been kicked out of their house. As family life is a central issue for homeless LGBTQ+ youth, some programs help families work toward acceptance and reunification.

Other relatives can also harass teens. All siblings fight. Some take it too far and become bullies. They may have power over their sibling because they are older, or because they have parental approval when their sibling does not.

If a teen is rejected by their family, they are more likely to struggle with mental health problems. They are more likely to become a victim of bullying at school. Bullying at home does not always stay in the family.

Bullies in the Community

Unfortunately, teens encounter many bullies outside of their home and school. Sometimes school bullies continue their behavior off campus. They may hound a victim at public places like the mall or on public transportation. If they live in their victim's

Bullying makes any setting feel hostile and unwelcoming. It can keep kids from enjoying the activities they want to pursue.

neighborhood, it may be hard to get away from them. All of these places could also have adults who bully LGBTQ+ teens, perhaps because they disapprove of LGBTQ+ people.

Teens may attend a community program or be on a community sports team with bullies. The bullies could be fellow participants or even the staff. Teens whose families practice a specific religion, especially one that does not support sexual and gender diversity, may encounter bullying at places of worship. Health care providers who are not sensitive to gender and sexuality issues may bully.

Teens who work a job or hold an internship might encounter workplace bullying. Bullying bosses can interfere with someone's ability to do their job. If the teen hasn't held a job before, constant criticism may make them doubt their worth as an employee. Bullying makes it hard to succeed. A bullied employee may feel like they won't be able to get a reference for another job.

An LGBTQ+ teen may be bullied in one setting by one person, or they may be bullied in different settings by a range of people. Just as being bullied at home makes a teen more likely to be bullied at school, bullied students are more likely to become bullied employees.

MYTHS AND FACTS

Myth: Bullying only happens at school.

Fact: While much of the focus on bullying has been in schools, teens can be bullied anywhere, by anyone. All a bully needs is power over someone else and the intent to cause harm.

Myth: People in the LGBTQ+ community don't bully.

Fact: Members of the LGBTQ+ community can also be bullies. Even those who face prejudice themselves can treat others badly.

Myth: Bullying is just a normal part of growing up.

Fact: Not all teens report being bullied, and even if they did, such acts would still not be OK. Teens who are bullied are more likely to struggle with mental and physical health issues.

CHAPTER TWO

CYBERBULLYING: THE BULLY THAT NEVER SLEEPS

Technology has given people unlimited access to the world. At any time of day, from almost any location, they can reach out to family, friends, and strangers. On the downside, technology also gives bullies the same freedom to attack their victims at any time and from anywhere.

Cyberbullying is a series of aggressive acts using technology. It can happen over the internet or using text messages. Cyberbullying shares many features with its real-world counterpart. Bullies cyberbully for the same reasons they participate in any kind of bullying. They are looking for attention or to make themselves more popular. They may enjoy having power or control over someone. They may also do it just because they can.

At first glance, cyberbullying might seem easy to stop—just stay away from the internet. However, staying offline is not an option for most teens. Technology has become a huge part of our lives, useful for everything from socializing to homework. Avoiding it cuts someone off from the good as well as the bad. Nor does turning off one's own device keep other people from seeing the attacks that cyberbullies have made on their victims.

Although hurtful comments can be made in person, technology gives bullying extra impact by making those abusive words harder to escape and easier to spread.

An Old Problem in a New Medium

A person who would otherwise not have the power to bully in person might bully in cyberspace. There they can act without worrying about being confronted, at least not right away. They might have power by being more tech savvy than their victim.

Anyone who is bullying may continue that campaign through technology. When a parent constantly criticizes their child in person, he can easily pick up a device and continue to criticize with texts. Siblings and peers from school can easily find their victim online through social media. Bosses may send threatening messages during work or after hours.

While much cyberbullying is a continuation of real-world bullying, some comes from strangers. Thanks to technology, users can meet people who live anywhere. The strangers may be participants in a chat room or online gaming. The strangers might stumble onto a teen's social media page that is public, or convince a teen to add them to their friends list. Some of these strangers may decide to become bullies.

Like other kinds of bullying, cyberbullying targets LGBTQ+ teens more than straight teens. In 2013, GLSEN found that 49 percent of the LGBTQ+ students they surveyed reported being electronically bullied in the past year. In 2015, 28 percent of lesbian, gay, and bisexual teens surveyed by the CDC reported being electronically bullied over the last year, versus 14.2 percent of straight students. Of the students who were unsure of their sexuality, 22.5 percent reported being cyberbullied.

CYBERCRIME

Cyberbullying can be a crime. State laws may specifically target cyberbullying, or the behavior itself may break other laws. Sometimes the actions count as hate crimes. Hate crimes are crimes motivated by prejudice against the target. In some states and situations, hate crime laws cover harassment based on sexual orientation or gender identity.

Repeated harassment of someone with the intent to cause fear may qualify as stalking. Cyberbullies can also break the law by threatening violence or by invading a target's privacy. It's illegal to take a photo or video of another person at a time or place they would reasonably expect privacy.

Some illegal photos were first taken by the victims themselves and sexted. Sending sexual messages and photos is risky for any teen. People who share sexual photos of underage youths can be charged with child pornography.

Poisoning the Web

Cyberbullying consists of both attacks aimed at victims and attacks on their reputation and relationships. Bullies might threaten, insult, or impersonate their target. Only physical bullying is not represented, although cyberbullying can include physical threats. The vast array of ways to communicate and share online means that cyberbullying may take many different forms. As technology evolves, the diversity of attacks will only increase.

Cyberbullies may send texts, instant messages, or emails. To gain an audience, they may forward or otherwise share these messages. They may attack their victims in chat rooms or on social media. If a teen plays online games, a bully might target them during the play, even encouraging others to gang up on them. The bullying may make it difficult to keep playing. Other acts of social exclusion can happen online, for example if a person is blocked from chat rooms or buddy lists.

Although most teens rely on technology for their schoolwork and social lives, for those who are cyberbullied it can be a source of pain and anxiety.

The messages may include embarrassing personal information, whether real or invented. The real information may have been discovered through electronic means. A victim may be hacked or tricked into revealing too much online. Their LGBTQ+ identity may be outed or spread across social media, whether they want it to be or not. Hackers might alter or delete files on the victim's computer or infect the computer with a virus. Bullies can also spread viruses by sending malicious codes or links.

Some teens sext, which is sending sexually explicit material through technology, usually to someone they are involved with or interested in. Sometimes teens send sexual photos of themselves. Bullies may get a hold of these messages or pictures and share them. The bully may even be a current or former love interest who was sent the material in the first place. The bully may take other embarrassing videos or pictures of the victim without their consent.

Cyberbullies sometimes impersonate their victims. They set up a fake profile and engage in embarrassing or improper behavior online. Or they create an embarrassing website. If a bully obtains a target's passwords, the bully may impersonate them using their real accounts. The bully may lock them out, making it harder to stop the bullying

Cyberbullies may create their own web pages dedicated to attacking or embarrassing their victim. The content may encourage visitors to contribute their own material or otherwise participate. For example, cyberbullies may set up an insulting web-based survey. Cyberbullies are limited only by their imagination, technology, their fear of being caught, and their conscience.

CYBERBULLYING AND SUICIDE

Does cyberbullying cause suicide? There have been several cases in the media in which incidents of cyberbullying appeared to do just that. The reality is more complex. There's no evidence that cyberbullying by itself was to blame. The victims in the media cases suffered from other risk factors that contributed to their tragedy.

Although cyberbullying does not seem to lead directly to suicide, the two can be related. Being involved in bullying can increase the risk that a teen engages in suicide-related behaviors, such as thinking about and planning suicide. It increases the likelihood a teen suffers anxiety and depression, which are also risk factors. However, most cyberbullied teens do not commit suicide. Even those at risk for suicide-related behaviors can find help to feel better. Suicide hotlines such as the Trevor Project's Lifeline (866-488-7386), which offers support for the LGBTQ+ community, are one place to turn for help.

From the Virtual to the Real World

While cyberbullying can have long-term consequences for everyone involved, in the short run technology makes the act of bullying easier on the bully and harder on the target. The bully doesn't take physical risks by confronting someone in person. They don't have to see the pain they cause. Witnessing pain can cause us to feel compassion. When a bully feels compassion for their victim, it can make them stop their hurtful behavior. With cyberbullying, the hurt is out of sight and often out of mind.

Cyberbullies can feel their own anger or dislike toward the target more strongly in an electronic setting. Other internet users may add to the cyberbullying, or add messages that show approval of the cyberbully's actions. When people pile on to attack the target, cyberbullies feel their emotions are justified. The bullies, not the victims, can end up feeling supported.

Teens can egg each other on when they cyberbully, which can lead to them intensifying their harassment, causing great harm to their victims.

Cyberbullying is so easy that people can act on a whim. Bullies might not take the time to think through the consequences for themselves or for others. They may assume there will be no personal consequences. Internet postings can seem anonymous. When someone is anonymous, their identity is hidden.

Anonymity feels powerful. Victims feel powerless because there is no one to confront. In addition, stepping away from the abuse is hard. Victims may feel lonely or worry they'll miss something important if they turn off their devices.

Even unplugging might not solve the problem. The material stays out there. Victims don't know who is looking at it, whether it's fellow students, family members, or even complete strangers. Even deleting material does not guarantee that it's gone. People may have made copies or screen shots. Attacks can lie in wait on the web or on someone's computer. The target may think their embarrassing photo is gone, only to encounter it months after the original incident.

Cyberbullying can have serious consequences for the bullies. While cyberbullies sometimes think their posts are anonymous, law enforcement and service providers have ways to track their source. Some forms of cyberbullying break the law and can lead to legal actions. Some schools include cyberbullying in their antibullying policies even though the behavior is off campus.

CHAPTER THREE

SELF-DEFENSE FOR TARGETS

B ullies make it hard for victims to feel good about themselves. Sometimes the people in the target's life don't make
things easier. They may suggest ignoring the bully, which
is hard to do when a bully has started a campaign of harassment
that might include attacks behind the target's back. Some unsym-
pathetic people may imply that the bullying is harmless or
somehow the target's fault.

If a teen is being bullied, it's important to remember that they
do not deserve to be treated this way. Even if they engaged in
unsafe behavior, the bully had no right to take advantage of those
mistakes. No one deserves to be harassed. A victim may feel help-
less to change their situation, but there are things that can be done.

Finding Allies

One of the best ways to start dealing with being bullied is by
reaching out to allies. A bully will try to keep their target isolated. But many people have the power and desire to support the
victim. Some they might already know, some they'll find in their
community, and some they might find online.

Victims of bullying should consider what adults in their life
might be sympathetic. It doesn't have to be a teacher or counselor. Family members or religious leaders might work. The adult

Bullied teens who lack close friendships may feel doubly isolated, but allies can be found at home, online, and in the community.

may be LGBTQ+ themselves, or they may be a straight ally. A straight ally does not identify as LGBTQ+ but supports LGBTQ+ equality. Some adults have power or influence that might lead to a change in the situation. Sometimes, however, an adult can help best by listening.

Adults are not the only option. Teens can reach out to people their own age, such as friends or siblings. Just spending time with friends fights the isolation created by bullying, even if the teen doesn't talk about their problems. Talking things out, though, can help victims better understand their experience and their feelings about it.

Friends can help victims strategize. A friend might help brainstorm options. They might accompany a victim when the victim talks to an adult. For those who are considering reporting the bullying, friends can help figure out the necessary steps.

Maybe the bully's target doesn't know anyone supportive of the LGBTQ+ community. If that's the case, they can look for LGBTQ+ support groups in school, in the community, or online.

This photo shows a cisgender teen (*left*) talking with a transgender teen in a high school in Johnson City, Kansas. Gay-Straight Alliances are a great place for teens of any gender or sexuality to make new friends.

gay-straight alliances are school clubs that allow students to socialize, discuss LGBTQ+ issues, and support each other. In general, the best community- and online-based groups for teens are ones that already have other teenage members.

Internet users should be careful with what they share online. Don't share sensitive photos or secrets. Never give out passwords to anyone, even friends. Former friends can become bullies.

Teens may feel uncomfortable reaching out to anyone in their life or community. Either they worry others won't be supportive, or they feel unable to take the risk. During these times, contacting a crisis line may help. It's vital for victims to reach out if they are worried for their safety or feeling suicidal. But even if they're just unsure what to do next, the person on the other end can help them sort through their options. Some crisis numbers such as the Trevor Lifeline (866-488-7386) are open all hours of the day. The Trevor Lifeline is staffed by counselors trained in supporting young people in crisis or looking for support. Some crisis lines have instant messaging and texting options.

Protecting the Victim

Targets of bullying should never respond in kind. Aggression can make the situation worse. When victims act aggressively toward a bully, the bully's behavior may escalate rather than stop. The bully may feel threatened and attack physically, even if the attacks were only verbal before. The bully might stop in-person bullying, but target their victim in cyberspace.

Targets who try to bully or fight their tormentor may end up being the one to get into trouble. Adults often don't know what led up to a situation. If the bully claims to be the victim, they might be believed. Even if such actions work in the short run, victims who bully may end up feeling worse about themselves in the long run.

Victims of bullying should stand up for themselves safely. If they confront a bully in person, it's vital to act assertive rather than aggressive. Assertive behavior is confident and firm without attacking or becoming emotional. In a clear, calm voice the victim can tell the bully that their behavior is not okay. Use the person's name and meet their eyes. Cyberbullying can also be countered assertively, rather than by engaging in a flame war.

Assertive behavior doesn't come easily to everyone. Allies can help. Victims may practice being assertive through role-playing. Friends may be willing to accompany a victim while they stand up to a bully.

Whatever the teen decides to do, the first order of business is to stay safe. If they can't be assertive, or if being assertive isn't working, they must get away from any dangerous situation. They should walk away to somewhere safe. In addition, they should try to avoid situations where they are alone with bullies. They can use internet and phone settings to control how cyberbullies can contact them.

When bullying is too overwhelming for teens to think clearly about solutions, it may be time to take a break. To escape a toxic home life, a teen might stay over at someone else's house for a while. If someone at work is bullying them, they can take vacation time or consider a new job. A break may give the victim a new perspective on their situation. If nothing else, they will appreciate the temporary relief.

Dealing with harassment may require making difficult choices. Teens should think carefully before deciding to change schools or leave home.

Teens who are bullied by their family might think about moving out. Before doing this, the teen should consider their options carefully. There are programs that help families better understand their LGBTQ+ children. If the teen is determined to leave, they should look for alternatives to living alone or being homeless, such as by living at a friend or relative's house.

When, and How, to Report

If a teen is being bullied, they should always consider telling someone about the incident. Whether they should formally report the behavior is a different question. It's a smart idea to discuss the issue with an ally. They can help the victim decide who they should report to and what they hope will come of the report. Together they can figure out what the reporting process involves.

When caregivers bully, the actions could be child abuse if they have a physical or sexual component. Emotional abuse is harder to prove since there needs to be evidence of harm. Child abuse or maltreatment can be reported to Child Protective Services or to the local police.

Organizations may have their own policies about bullying. The behavior can also be reported to someone who is responsible for the bully's behavior. For community groups, this may be staff or administrators. On the job, the report can go to the bully's boss or, if the company has one, the human resources department. Victims may have to go outside of the company to be heard. The US Equal Employment Opportunity Commission covers discrimination based on sexual orientation or gender identity. State laws may also apply.

MAKING A TRAIL

Being bullied is upsetting. When targets try to talk to someone or report the behavior, they may have trouble remembering details. Having a written or electronic record to refer to can help. If the target wants to report the behavior, this record helps them make their case.

For each instance of bullying, the target should take down when it happened, who was there, and what exactly happened. Every detail of the interaction is important. While there may be no witnesses to many instances of in-person bullying—or the witnesses may decline to speak—technology makes cyberbullying easy to record. When being cyberbullied, the target can save messages and take screen shots of the abuse.

Victims can report cyberbullying in various ways depending on who is doing it and what they are doing. Bullying behavior may break terms of service for social media or internet providers.

If another student is behind the attacks, their school's antibullying policy might address cyberbullying. A sympathetic teacher can help a victim determine how to report the incidents. Be aware that a teacher may be required to report bullying when they find out about it.

When cyberbullying appears to include criminal acts, it can be reported to the police. It doesn't matter if the attacks are anonymous. The authorities can usually find the culprit and possibly

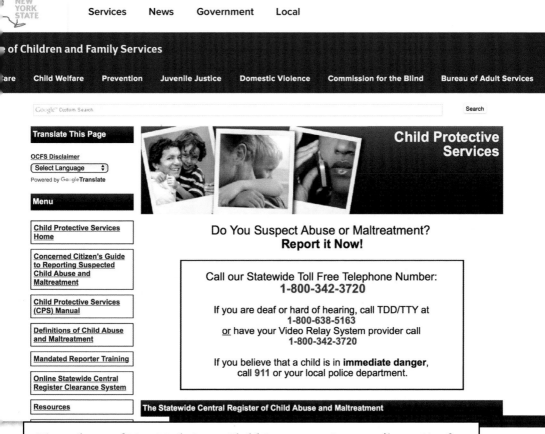

The website of New York State Child Protective Services (http://ocfs .ny.gov/main/cps) is shown above. Teens who feel they are experiencing abuse or neglect can find help from the similar agency in their state.

uncover evidence that's been deleted. For example, most web posts can be traced to an IP address. Cell phone companies can recover the content of texts.

Before or after reporting the attack, the victim can ask what will happen next. Will there be an investigation or mediation? Will officials follow up with the victim after a certain amount of time? If no progress is being made, they can contact whomever they reported it to and ask what's being done.

10 GREAT QUESTIONS TO ASK A GUIDANCE COUNSELOR

1. Does my specific experience qualify as bullying?

2. Does my school have an antibullying policy?

3. Does that policy include bullying that a student engages in off campus?

4. Does the policy include cyberbullying?

5. Are LGBTQ+ issues mentioned in the policy?

6. How do I report the type of bullying I'm experiencing?

7. What should I expect out of the reporting process?

8. Is there a LGBTQ+ support group at my school?

9. Does my school have the resources to help families support their LGBTQ+ children?

10. Does my school have a counselor who can help me recover from bullying?

CHAPTER FOUR

CHALLENGING THE CULTURE OF BULLYING

Sadly, some people think it's OK to target others for being LGBTQ+. Society in general has made great progress in terms of accepting sexual and gender minorities, but not everyone has kept up. Some public figures say hateful things about sexual and gender minorities. Some religions condemn the LGBTQ+ community. Teachers may be prevented by school policies from addressing LGBTQ+ issues.

People also learn to value bullying behavior. Characters in shows and movies act in cruel ways to get laughs. Parents may have experienced aggressive parenting styles when they were children and continue the cycle with their own children. Breaking these patterns may require learning to value kindness and compassion.

The culture of bullying can be fought by increasing tolerance for people who are different and by decreasing the acceptance of bullying behavior.

Educating for Tolerance

Bullies who target LGBTQ+ people may think their family and community agree with their actions. Bystanders and family members may wrongly believe that the victim brought the bullying on themselves. These family members and bystanders might think that if only LGBTQ+ teens would conform to society's expectations, they wouldn't be harassed.

People fear and hate what they do not understand. So understanding is one of the best roads to tolerance. A lot of misinformation floats around, even among LGBTQ+ people. Lesbian and gay people may not understand the needs of youth with minority gender identities. Bisexuals face misunderstanding from all sides.

When people learn about LGBTQ+ issues and get to know people from the community, they become less likely to target LGBTQ+ people. They may even speak out against intolerance when they see it. Education campaigns show that community

This photo from 2015 shows an LGBTQ+ Pride Parade in Birmingham, England. The LGBTQ+ community has gained many rights, but there is still work to be done to achieve full equality.

leaders and others value and support the diverse identities of people in their community.

It's important that antibullying policies specifically mention sexual and gender diversity. Otherwise teens may think that bullying in general is not okay, but that the community will turn a blind eye when the targets are LGBTQ+.

While the community needs education about sexual and gender diversity, people running a campaign should consider covering other kinds of diversity as well. No one deserves to be attacked for their race, ethnicity, religion, or abilities, any more than they deserve to be attacked for being LGBTQ+.

In fact, no one deserves to be bullied, no matter their identity. The best antibullying programs teach social skills, empathy, and inclusion to everyone. Aggressive and cruel behavior makes an environment toxic for all community and family members. It doesn't just affect people directly involved in bullying.

Getting the Message Out

Schools often run antibullying campaigns, but so do community organizations. Consider approaching libraries and community centers, for example. Libraries serve the greater community and strive to be welcoming to everyone. Many library collections already include resources about bullying, the LGBTQ+ community, and positive parenting. Places of worship can get involved. While some religions teach against sexual and gender minorities, others preach tolerance or even embrace their LGBTQ+ members.

Companies can support a community campaign or bring education directly to their own employees. They can require their workers to attend diversity or antiharassment training. Workplaces covered by federal laws against discrimination are required to post information about those laws. They can also put up posters affirming their commitment to diversity.

What a campaign looks like is up to the people who run it. Organizations can provide a variety of reading material to the public, from books and pamphlets to blogs. A campaign could be as simple as a library displaying books and movies on bullying and the LGBTQ+ community in a visible place. Places of worship could offer literature that argues for tolerance from a religious standpoint.

A more direct way to bring the community together is by organizing events. Speakers could talk about their experiences with bullying or the LGBTQ+ community. Workshops could teach positive parenting techniques or assertiveness. Libraries and community centers might consider making online safety classes an ongoing offering. The events could include a film series that mixes fun movies about LGBTQ+ people with documentaries and antibullying videos. Movies can entertain and educate at the same time.

Having an online component to a campaign is a way to use the power of technology for good. An online campaign might provide a way for people in the community to share their stories or give others their support. This can happen with a message board, comment page, or hashtag, for example.

An online campaign may give links to informative websites, to supportive organizations, or to local safe spaces. Safe spaces

Activist Chris Maliwat is introduced at the 2009 National Conference on LGBT Equality in San Francisco, California. Maliwat spoke about his efforts to oppose Proposition 8, a 2008 law, later overturned, that

are places meant for people to be open about their sexuality and gender without fearing harassment. They are usually designated with a sign that might include a triangle, rainbow, or both.

Whoever is running the campaign should consider how to moderate online spaces. Bullies should not be able to use them to mock victims of bullying, the LGBTQ+ community, or other minorities. The goal of a campaign is to increase tolerance, not to give bullies a wider audience.

BYSTANDER POWER

Bystanders are a big part of bullying. Although teen bullies often avoid acting in front of adults who might stop them, they usually want the attention of peers. Gaining power or popularity requires witnesses. Bullies can be egged on or joined by other bullies. But even when bystanders watch silently, the bullies can feel supported.

Not only are bystanders sucked in to the dynamics of bullying, but they can also be affected by what they see. Bullying makes them more likely than kids who do not witness bullying to have mental health problems. They feel less safe.

Fortunately, bystanders are powerful. A brief statement from a bystander can sometimes stop bullying. A bystander may worry about becoming the next target, but they can have a positive impact even without confronting the bully if they focus on the victim.

A bystander can help the victim get to a safe place, if the bullying is happening in person and they can do so safely. It's important for a bystander to say supportive and positive things about the victim whenever there is a chance. The bystander can post positive comments about the victim online or spend time with them after the incident. Doing so will combat their feelings of isolation and loneliness.

Turning Bullying Families into Supportive Families

Some family members who bully don't know any better. They think they are helping their teen by trying to keep them straight.

They don't see the damage that their bullying causes. These family members may be open to education. They may learn to support their LGBTQ+ teen when they better understand their loved one's situation and needs.

This education may come from literature, from another adult whom they respect, or through an organization. If they are religious, they may appreciate talking to someone who practices a religion that supports sexual and gender minorities. They may find it helpful to interact with people who had to overcome their own intolerance before becoming a straight ally.

Some family members may be willing to attend meetings of support groups like PFLAG. PFLAG is a national group with chapters throughout the United States and sister organizations based internationally. PFLAG is dedicated to uniting straight people, especially family and friends of LGBTQ+ people, with the LGBTQ+ community.

The process of coming to acceptance takes time. Some family members won't try. But when families are willing to work against their prejudices, they signal their commitment to their LGBTQ+ family members. Their efforts will begin the work of healing their relationship with their loved one.

Rules of Engagement

Sometimes adults are so focused on whether a behavior counts as bullying that they do not address bad behavior because it might not qualify as bullying. When the community supports or ignores these unacceptable types of behaviors, all young people suffer.

Stopping bullying requires more than punishing bullies. The culture needs to change. Teens and adults need to know that antisocial behaviors like aggression, cruelty, and social exclusion are not acceptable. If the behavior is never okay, then bystanders and teachers can call out small acts even when they aren't sure bullying is occurring.

People participating in community programs, such as clubs and sports, or those belonging to a family unit can agree on acceptable ways to behave towards each other. These behavioral expectations should be explicit and include tolerance of diversity. Members should also be expected to practice kindness and cooperation with each other. Behavioral expectations won't solve cases of severe harassment, but it can discourage people from starting to bully or escalating their behavior. It also empowers bystanders to say something.

People can come to their agreement in different ways. Teens could ask their family to set up a family meeting. They might ask a supportive relative for help, even if the relative isn't in their household. The relative might be willing to help plan or attend the meeting.

Community spaces can post expectations for how people will behave toward each other. Teens might have to sign an agreement before they participate in a program. If not, approach leaders and directors at the organization about creating these expectations. For a community program, time can be set aside in the beginning to let participants brainstorm ideas or otherwise discuss the expectations together.

Sometimes parents who love their LGBTQ+ teens need help learning to accept their children for who they are rather than trying to change them.

Expectations for online behavior can be made clear. Moderators and members can post rules for comments on blogs, chat rooms, or online groups. If you're not in charge of an online group, get permission from other members so that everyone agrees to the guidelines.

CHAPTER FIVE

HEALING THE WOUNDS

Even if a teen is no longer being bullied, some damage has been done. They may feel isolated and distrustful of others, and develop low self-esteem. They may feel unhappy about being LGBTQ+. They may feel foolish if they've made themselves vulnerable online and struggle with both mental and physical health issues.

Being bullied is not the victim's fault. No matter who they are or what they did, someone else made the decision to target them. It doesn't mean something is wrong with the teen. Most LGBTQ+ people will grow into healthy adults despite the challenges they've faced. So can they.

First Aid for Mental Health

Victims of bullying are more likely than other teens to struggle with mental health issues such as anxiety and depression. They are more likely to think about suicide. If a teen is worried about harming themselves, they should seek help immediately. Talk to someone you trust such as a teacher, family member, or friend. Or contact a crisis line.

If they are in a serious crisis, they can get help at an emergency room. Otherwise, they can find a mental health professional. It's important to look for a counselor or therapist supportive of the LGBTQ+ community. Teens need someone who will help

Mental health issues, such as anxiety and depression, can happen to anyone and are not a sign of weakness. Like other illnesses, mental health problems can be treated.

them grow, not a person who will question their identity and narrow their options. Ideally they should talk to someone with training and experience in mental health and LGBTQ+ issues.

Seeking help does not show weakness. All of us have problems we can't solve ourselves, or that we could use help facing. Even teens who are not in crisis can talk with therapists and counselors to better understand their experiences and how those experiences affected them. For some issues, medication may help along with talk therapy.

CHALLENGING NEGATIVE THOUGHTS

Anxiety or depression can lead to an overwhelming flood of **negative thoughts**. These thoughts might question a person's worth, popularity, abilities, or even their right to happiness. The mind continues to bring up evidence supporting negative beliefs while ignoring the positive things in their life. Worries can consume anxious people. Negative thinking becomes a habit and affects how people act in all areas of their life.

Therapy can make a difference. Cognitive behavior therapy is one kind of therapy that gives people the tools to confront negative thoughts and the behaviors that come with them. Through talking with a therapist, patients learn to identify their negative patterns. By identifying these patterns, people have the chance to challenge them.

The process takes work. For example, some worries involve a specific concern that's real. Life always has a degree of uncertainty. But coping with realistic concerns is easier than coping with general, overwhelming worries. People can learn to replace negative thoughts with more realistic self-talk. With help, people can free themselves from the behaviors that are keeping them from living healthier, happier lives.

Counseling sessions may happen individually, with the teen talking to the counselor alone. Teens may also meet in a group of patients with the counselor leading the therapy. If issues at home are important, teens might attend family therapy with their parents and siblings.

When the targets of bullying turn to substance abuse, they may need professional help to stop. Not only are these substances addictive, using them may be a way to avoid feeling the effects of

Art can help people express emotions that are otherwise hard to access. You don't need special skills or great talent to benefit from creating art.

bullying. Doctors can help teens find counseling or a treatment program that works for them.

Not all help must be professional. In conversations with supportive adults or peers, bullied teens can process their experiences along with their feelings and continuing challenges. Art is another great outlet for expression. A teen can write about what happened to them, for example, or draw a picture illustrating their emotions. There's no need to worry about talent or technique or sharing the work with others. Just the act of making art can help.

Reclaiming Life

As bad as bullying is, it's only one small part of life. A teen who has been the victim of bullying is so much more than a target. One way to reclaim their life from bullying is to remember things they enjoy. What kinds of books, movies, music, and games do they appreciate? Do they have any hobbies? Would they like some? The internet can be a great source of activity ideas and how-to videos, not just a way for someone to be bullied.

New things can be more fun when sampled with other people. Teens can take a class or join a group with youths doing something they think they'd enjoy. Maybe they've always wanted to go camping, practice martial arts, or play Dungeons and Dragons. This is a great way to meet new friends while learning new skills.

One way to combat feeling like a victim is by helping others in need or by contributing to a cause. Volunteer activities that help people or animals are healing. Or they can join a group working towards a goal they care about. What issues in the local

A teen who has endured cruelty and harassment may find relief in experiencing the unconditional love of animals, whether at home or through volunteering at a shelter.

community do they find important? These areas of interest don't have to be LGBTQ+ related.

Having activities away from their bullies can increase their confidence. But be aware that being the target of bullying can make someone feel more anxious in new situations. They may worry someone they meet will turn into a bully. One way to calm those fears is to discuss them with an ally ahead of time. The teen can consider inviting a friend along so they already know at least one person.

It's important for teens who have been bullied to have fun, but they also need to take care of their physical health. It's hard to feel good while being unhealthy. They need to get enough sleep each night as exhaustion worsens a person's ability to deal with challenges. Eating a healthy diet is vital, including food they enjoy. Cooking can be confidence-building as well as tasty. The internet is full of tips on cooking healthy meals and making healthy snacks. They can cook by themselves, with friends, or with family members.

Being physically active gives teens more energy, relieves stress, and promotes a better relationship between the person and their

When you're being bullied, it's hard to find joy in life. Connecting with nature while staying active can help you gain energy and manage stress.

body. Try to break up screen time by getting up and moving. Learn some stretching exercises or yoga poses. There's no need for an intense workout. If they prefer, they can go dancing or take a long walk. Getting out in nature feeds the soul.

LGBTQ+ Pride

Anyone who has experienced bullying can benefit from taking care of their mental and physical health. But LGBTQ+ teens need support for their identity as well. Without that affirmation, recovery is more difficult.

This is especially important for questioning youth. Bullying can make the process of exploring one's sexuality and gender much harder. Instead of enjoying the chance to discover things about themselves, questioning youths might worry about what is wrong with their identity.

To combat these negative feelings, seek out positive experiences of LGBTQ+ culture. One way to is through entertainment media. Librarians and websites can recommend books and movies with positive LGBTQ+ characters. Teens who have friends in the community might start an informal book group. Friends can also watch movies together.

Community LGBTQ+ groups and GSAs provide supportive environments for both questioning and non-questioning youths. Sometimes it feels reassuring for teens to be with people who understand their issues. Although people in the LGBTQ+ community differ from each other as much as anyone else, many share similar experiences related to their orientation and gender. Such groups might be a chance to meet potential romantic partners. Dating can be a way to explore and appreciate one's orientation.

Seeing well-adjusted LGBTQ+ adults can be reassuring if a youth is worried about always struggling. It may be helpful to get to know these LGBTQ+ adults outside of a group setting. Spend time with an LGBTQ+ mentor. A mentor is an experienced and trusted person who can help with guidance and understanding. A supportive teacher or parent may be able to find an adult in the community who would be open to friendship with a teen.

Both straight allies and LGBTQ+ people may have gone through their own period of questioning even if they are certain of their identity now. Talking with them may help a youth clarify their own identity. Or it may reassure a teen to realize that there's nothing wrong with being in a place of not knowing. Questioning takes time.

Ultimately, questioning youth may realize they are straight and that their gender conforms to the one they were assigned at birth. There's nothing wrong with that. Every individual must discover who they are. For some people, that means embracing an LGBTQ+ identity. For others, it doesn't. Nor do they have to stick to any decision they make now. Teens may revisit their questions in the future.

An LGBTQ+ teen's path is theirs and theirs alone. No matter where it takes them, they deserve to follow it without the fear of other people harassing them. But if they are being bullied at home or in the community, it's important to know that they can beat it.

ANONYMOUS With one's name or identity unknown.

ASEXUAL Being uninterested in sex, although not necessarily uninterested in romance.

ASSERTIVE Expressing oneself in a confident and firm manner.

BISEXUAL Sexually, emotionally, or romantically attracted to more than one gender.

CISGENDER Having a gender identity that matches the gender they were assigned at birth.

CYBERBULLY Someone who uses technology to bully.

GAY-STRAIGHT ALLIANCE A student-run club whose members discuss issues related to gender and sexuality.

GENDER EXPRESSION The way people conver their gender to the world.

GENDER FLUID Having a gender identity that changes over time.

GENDER IDENTITY The gender people see themselves as.

GENDERQUEER Identifying as neither male nor female or as some combination of the two.

HARASSMENT The act of continually tormenting or bothering someone.

HATE CRIMES Crimes motivated by prejudice against the victim.

HOMOPHOBIC Afraid of or biased against people attracted to the same sex.

IMPERSONATE To pretend to be someone else.

INTERSEX Born with physical characteristics of more than one sex.

LESBIAN Identifying as female and being sexually, romantically, or emotionally attracted to other females.

MENTOR A trusted and experienced person who can provide guidance and advice.

PANSEXUAL Having sexual, romantic, or emotional attraction to people unlimited by gender.

SEXTING Sending someone sexually explicit photos or messages using technology.

TRANSGENDER Having a gender identity or expression which doesn't match the gender one was assigned at birth.

TRANSPHOBIC Afraid of or biased against transgender people.

FOR MORE INFORMATION

Gay, Lesbian, And Straight Education Network
110 William Street, 30th Floor
New York, NY 10038
(212) 727-0135
Website: http://www.glsen.org/
GLSEN works to combat hostile school environments for
LGBTQ+ kids. The organization conducts research, develops
resources, and partners with students and organizations to
make positive change for all students.

It Gets Better Project
110 S. Fairfax Avenue, Suite A11-71
Los Angeles, CA 90036
Website: http://www.itgetsbetter.org/
The It Gets Better Project is dedicated to letting LGBTQ+ teens
know that they too can have a happy, healthy future. The
project offers tens of thousands of videos made by adults with
inspiring messages for youths.

Lesbian Gay Bi Trans Youth Line
PO Box 73118, Wood Street PO
Toronto, ON, M4Y 2W5
Canada
(800) 268-9688
Website: http://www.youthline.ca
The LGBT Youth Line provides support for LGBTQ+ youth, by
youth, in the Ontario, Canada region.

PFLAG Canada
251 Bank St. 2nd floor
Ottawa, ON, K2P 1X3
Canada
(888) 530-6777
Website: http://pflagcanada.ca
PFLAG Canada provides support for Canadians dealing with
    LGBTQ+ issues. They provide information and education
    particularly for families struggling with acceptance of
    LGBTQ+ children.

The Trevor Project
PO Box 69232
West Hollywood, CA 90069
(866) 488-7386
Website: http://www.thetrevorproject.org
The Trevor Project runs the Trevor Lifeline, a crisis and sui-
    cide-prevention hotline for LGBTQ+ youths, which is
    available 24/7.

Websites

Because of the changing nature of internet links, Rosen Publishing
has developed an online list of websites related to the subject of
this book. This site is updated regularly. Please use this link to
access the list:

http://www.rosenlinks.com/LGBTQG/bully

FOR RURTHER READING

Belge, Kathy and Marke Bieschke. *Queer: The Ultimate LGBT Guide for Teens*. San Francisco, CA: Zest Books, 2011.

Huegel, Kelly. *GLBTQ: The Survival Guide for Gay, Lesbian, Bisexual, Transgender, and Questioning Teens*. 2nd ed. Minneapolis, MN: Free Spirit Publishing, 2011.

Kamberg, Mary-Lane. *I Have Been Bullied. Now What?* New York, NY: Rosen Publishing, 2015.

Kuklin, Susan. *Beyond Magenta: Transgender Teens Speak Out*. Somerville, MA: Candlewick Press, 2015.

Lohmann, Raychelle Cassada and Julia V. Taylor. *The Bullying Workbook for Teens: Activities to Help You Deal with Social Aggression and Cyberbullying*. Oakland, CA: Instant Help, 2013.

McAneney, Caitie. *I Have Been Cyberbullied. Now What?* New York, NY: Rosen Publishing, 2016.

Michaels, Vanessa, and Jeremy Harrow. *Frequently Asked Questions About Family Violence*. New York, NY: Rosen Publishing, 2012.

Peterson, Judy Monroe. *How to Beat Cyberbullying*. New York, NY: Rosen Publishing, 2013.

Savage, Dan and Terry Miller, eds. It Gets Better: *Coming Out, Overcoming Bullying, and Creating a Life Worth Living*. New York, NY: Penguin Books, 2012.

Testa, Rylan Jay, Deborah Coolhart, and Jayme Peta. *The Gender Quest Workbook: A Guide for Teens and Young Adults Exploring Gender Identities*. Oakland, CA: Instant Help, 2015.

BIBLIOGRAPHY

Center for Disease Control and Prevention. "Child Abuse and Neglect: Prevention Strategies." April 5, 2016. http://www .cdc.gov/violenceprevention/childmaltreatment/prevention .html.

Child Welfare Information Gateway. "What Is Child Abuse and Neglect? Recognizing the Signs and Symptoms." Children's Bureau, 2013. https://www.childwelfare.gov/pubPDFs /whatiscan.pdf.

Englander, Elizabeth Kandel. *Bullying and Cyberbullying: What Every Educator Needs to Know*. Cambridge, MA: Harvard Education Press, 2013.

Durso, Laura E., and Gary J. Gates. "Serving Our Youth: Findings from a National Survey of Services Providers Working with Lesbian, Gay, Bisexual and Transgender Youth Who Are Homeless or at Risk of Becoming Homeless." The Williams Institute with True Colors Fund and the Palette Fund, 2012. http://escholarship.org/uc/item /80x75033#page-1.

Hoetger, Lori A., Katherine P. Hazen, Eve M. Brank. "All in the Family: A Retrospective Study Comparing Sibling Bullying and Peer Bullying." *Journal of Family Violence*, 30(2015): 103–111. http://digitalcommons.unl.edu/cgi/viewcontent .cgi?article=1015&context=ccflfacpub.

Human Rights Campaign. "Growing up LGBT in America: HRC Youth Survey Report Key Findings." Human Righst Campaign, 2012. http://hrc-assets.s3-website-us-east-1 .amazonaws.com//files/assets/resources/Growing-Up-LGBT

-in-America_Report.pdf.

Kann, Laura, and Emily O'Malley Olsen, Tim McManus, William H. Harris, Shari L. Shanklin, Katherine H. Flint, Barbara Queen, et al. "Sexual Identity, Sex of Sexual Contacts, and Health-Related Behaviors Among Students in Grades 9–12 – United States and Selected Sites, 2015." *MMWR Surveillance Summaries* 65 (2016): 1–202. http://www.cdc.gov/mmwr/volumes/65/ss/ss6509a1.htm.

Kosciw, Joseph G., and Emily A. Greytak, Neal A. Palmer, and Madelyn J. Boesen, "2013 National School Climate Survey: The Experiences of Lesbian, Gay, Bisexual and Transgender Youth in Our Nation's Schools." GLSEN, 2013. http://www.glsen.org/sites/default/files/2013%20National%20School%20Climate%20Survey%20Full%20Report_0.pdf.

National Institute on Drug Abuse. "What to Do if You Have a Problem with Drugs: For Teens and Young Adults." January 2016. https://www.drugabuse.gov/related-topics/treatment/what-to-do-if-you-have-problem-drugs-teens-young-adults.

Russel, Stephen T., and Jessica N. Fish. "Mental Health in Lesbian, Gay, Bisexual, and Transgender (LGBT) Youth." *Annual Review Clinical Psychology*, 12(2016):465–487. http://www.ncbi.nlm.nih.gov/pmc/articles/PMC4887282.

Schulman, Michael. "Generation LGBTQIA." *New York Times*, January 9, 2013. http://www.nytimes.com/2013/01/10/fashion/generation-lgbtqia.html?_r=0.

US Department of Health and Human Services. "Stopbullying.gov." Retrieved August 30, 2016. https://www.stopbullying.gov.

INDEX

H
harassment, 10, 21, 27, 41, 44
hate crimes, 21
homelessness, 14, 33
homophobia, 12
Human Rights Campaign, 10

L
lesbian, 6, 38
LGBTQ+ community, 4–7, 17, 24, 29, 37, 40
LGBTQ+ pride, 53–54
LGBTQ+ tolerance, 38–39, 40

P
PFLAG, 43

Q
queer, 6

R
reclaiming life after bullying, 50–53

S
self-defense, 27–30
sexting, 21, 23
sexual orientation, 5–6, 33
substance abuse, 10, 48–49
suicide, 24, 46
support, 29, 43

from community, 29–30, 39, 50
from family, 41–42, 44
from friends, 28–29, 43, 46, 53
online, 40
for victims

T
transgender, 6, 7, 12
transphobia, 12
Trevor Project Lifeline, 24, 30

About the Author

Clara MacCarald is a member of the LGBTQ+ community and an author with a master's degree in biology who writes educational books for children. She has also written about news and science for local publications in central New York. She belongs to the National Association of Science Writers and to the Society of Children's Book Writers and Illustrators.

Photo Credits

Cover, p. 1 SpeedKingz/Shutterstock.com; pp. 4–5 Chun Ju Wu/Alamy Stock Photo; p. 9 mrohana/iStock/Thinkstock; p. 11 Caroline Purser/Photographer's Choice/Getty Images; p. 12 Juanmonino/E+/Getty Images; pp. 15, 22 Fuse/Corbis/Getty Images; p. 19 Highwaystarz-Photography/iStock/Thinkstock; p. 25 Jon Feingersh/Blend Images/Getty Images; p. 28 gpointstudio/iStock/Thinkstock; p. 29 Kansas City Star/Tribune News Service/Getty Images; p. 32 Corbis/VCG/Getty Images; p. 38 Jemma Jones/Alamy Stock Photo; p. 41 Craig F. Walker/Denver Post/Getty Images; p. 45 Monkey Business Images/Shutterstock.com; p. 47 Monkey Business Images/Monkey Business/Thinkstock; p. 49 Yurriy/iStock/Thinkstock; p. 51 Camille Tokerud/The Image Bank/Getty Images; p. 52 Thomas Northcut/Digital Vision/Thinkstock; interior pages background (hands) Rawpixel.com/Shutterstock.com.

Designer: Nelson Sá; Editor: Jennifer Landau; Photo Researcher: Karen Huang